The Long Blue Room

JOAN GELFAND

The Long Blue Room
All Rights Reserved
Copyright @2014 Benicia Literary Arts
Published by Benicia Literary Arts
www.benicialiteraryarts.org
Benicia, California

ISBN 978-0-9703737-2-4
Library of Congress Control Number: 2013956287

Produced by Benicia Literary Arts, which encourages reading and writing in the community by producing events, creating a community of writers and readers, encouraging their development, and publishing works of high quality in all genres. The organization's website is www.BeniciaLiteraryArts.org.

Artistic Director - Gregory Berger, Pomegranate Design
Editing and layout by Lois Requist

Cover art used by permission
Vincent van Gogh (1853 - 1890)
The bedroom, 1888 Arles
oil on canvas, 72.4 x 91.3 cm
Van Gogh Museum, Amsterdam (Vincent van Gogh Foundation)
s47V/1962
F482

Also by
Joan Gelfand

Poetry:

Seeking Center
Two Bridges Press, 2006

A Dreamer's Guide To Cities and Streams
San Francisco Bay Press, 2009

Fiction:

Here & Abroad
Cervena Barva Press, 2010

CD:

Transported
Daveland Studios, 2011

For my Mother,
Jean Gelfand
8/18/1926-3/19/2010

*"The purpose of poetry is to remind us how
difficult it is to remain just one person,
for our house is open, there are no keys
in the doors, and invisible guests
come in and out at will."*

From "Ars Poetica" by Czselaw Milosz

CONTENTS

FOREWORD

"Sing to me of things you will not say,
In rhythm and rhyme,
Sing to me in three-quarter time."

This verse could stand as a *pars pro toto* for Joan Gelfand's new poetry
collection. It is the conclusion of the poem "Music: Dream Seven,"
addressing a lover, but it could as well be a love appeal to poetry itself,
speaking to the Muse – calling up her mystery, her playful dance, her craft.

Poem by poem, the same deceptive simplicity shines from the pages,
a confident, at times deliciously cocky confidence in her craft, the
elegance of rhythm, the musical phrasing. The tension for the poet
of the paradox *don't say!* finds its resolution in a playfully tossed
invitation to the dance.

This is what poetry does at its best: it sings what cannot be said, puts
a spell on what must not be spelled out. The poet makes the reader
(the lover) feel, taste, smell, hear, see in and around words. She takes
us into the realm of the senses, makes us long for "Paris Kisses" and
summer peaches, draws us into the light of a painting by Monet or
the sheltering blue of Van Gogh's room. Her melody is joyous,
provocative, bitter-sweet. Death is always nearby, always already in
the now – as in love, where "the ending is in the beginning."

This new collections of poems reveals a heart of seasoned wisdom,
looking at the suffering of nature and at human pain with unflinching
honesty. In the poem "Mother's Day" a woman throws herself in front
of a train:
But under the lights of 42nd Street
Something fell - luminous but odd
The shape an arm
A leg, like someone diving
Without grace
Into a deep pool.

The topography of *The Long Blue Room* is a vast panorama, from cities and streams to continents. San Francisco, New York, Santa Monica, Paris, Russian River vineyards, Mexico, Hawaii, California's wild beaches, the Metro, places of meditation, a moonless night, a lake, a breakfast table. Titles invite, entice. "Paris Whistling," "Ode to Toast." "Sex. Death. And All That Jazz," "Three Poems About Nothing," "Tassa Hanalei."

Joan Gelfand's formal mastery doesn't need many words. Haiku-like brevity allows time to stretch from a few lines into contemplation. Slightly longer poems launch into moods and modes with full velocity, only to unload their emotional tension, their spiritual, political charge in an unsuspected rhyme, a breath of recognition, a smile.

The sensuous love for life captured here, the formal assurance, the ease of words make this book a cherished companion, in a sense quite as simple and stunning as Gertrude Stein's, "I like the feeling of words doing as they want to do and as they have to do."

Renate Stendhal
Author: *Gertrude Stein: In Words and Pictures*
www.renatestendhal.com

INTRODUCTION

The Long Blue Room is the first work accepted by Benicia Literary
Arts for publication. We're excited to be a part of showcasing this
seasoned, eloquent poet.

Joan's work is firmly set in our world—with images we recognize and
places we see on a daily basis in California and in the daily news. Joan
considers the environmental impact of vineyards overtaking apple
orchards of the Russian River area. She meditates on the simple
pleasure of Toast, as in "Ode to Toast" and the delight of peaches
in "Bumper Crop."

Contemplating the meaning of love in the section "Sex. Death. And
All That Jazz," Joan questions: "Is it a simple affirmation of life in all
that emptiness?" (From "Making Love in an Empty Apartment.)"

In "Good Morning, America, Where Are You?" Joan tackles the
economic crisis, questioning our "faith in the Street" as so many have
been caught in the economic roiling of the last few years.

Finally, she asks us to see beyond the trivial, to consider love as
"…something mysterious…fleeting…and much more tender,"
in "La Dolce Vida."

Her work both celebrates and acknowledges the problems and
pleasures of today's world. With wry humor and insights into life in
our times, she invites us to share, enjoy, and participate in all that we
see and are.

Lois Requist
Poet Laureate
Benicia, California
2013

The Long Blue Room

GOOD MORNING, AMERICA, WHERE ARE YOU?

Now that the buck has stopped
The jig is up
The well run
Dry your eyes. You're done.

The party's over the game is played
The bad boys took off
With the cache.

Now that the buck has stopped
Where are you?
What's your place?
What's really on your mind?

Now that the buck has stopped
Did you make the right choices,
Sacrifice the best of times?
Can you remember your kid's last season?
Who won, who lost, who's behind?

Good morning America.
The drug of distraction has worn off
The cocaine high of overvalued
Done. Gone. Good-bye.

And this downturn, this turn down,
This big big disappointment, bummer slump
Might just be Nature's way of cooling us off
Cooling us down - all that dough
Rising and rising making us feel
Supernatural. But you know
She's the boss!
Nature had to cool off!
Man! She was feeling the heat.

You have lost and
I feel for you
All that hard work and
Faith in The Street.

There's a knock-knock joke
In here somewhere:
Something along the lines of
"How many Investment Managers
Does it take to screw...?"

Or was that greed
I heard knocking
Your knees back there?

Who Will Immortalize You?

Crowded Metro early Saturday evening
Gucci, Chanel, shined shoes, perfume.
Smartly dressed and coiffed, jostled by train's throttle
Families, coming home, contented babies sucking bottles,
Snuggled into strollers. Boulevardiers searching for fun.
And you, crumpled into corner. A sore thumb.

Tattered combat jacket, soiled shoes,
Stinking of piss, dark alleys and taverns
Lift your head as if from a well,
Tip a half-empty bottle to your lips, and sing.
Your voice, aligned with all that is boundless, heavenly:
Opera, starlit nights, your wife, Nanjing.

Your beautiful song is cut short.
An inner demon takes charge.
You kick the wall
Desperate to escape your private movie.

Who will immortalize you?

You, from the Russian Steppe perhaps, or Outer Mongolia?
That gorgeous place of quiet, in the mountains?

Which war killed your family? Was it tribal? political?
You were never immune.
You meet no one's eyes, remember the wine,
Suck another slug, hum another bar.

Who will immortalize you?

You, from the poorest province –
Airlifted out, a random act of kindness
Your home a memory. Your song, the thinnest thread
To stitch soul and life together.

The Long Blue Room (La Chambre a Arles)

"The frame - as there is no white in the picture - will be white. This by way of revenge for the enforced rest I was obliged to take."

Letter to Theo, 1888

Vincent, your long blue room
("Lilac," you called it) yellow spread
("Like butter,") the wicker chairs,
The rough-hewn dresser.
Through the shutters,
Provence's watery light.

You were just home,
Minus one lobe.
You wanted a respite
You painted the long blue room not once
But three times. You had to get it right.
The long blue room was your retreat
From working in a fever, a pique
A flurry of rejection.

I

nspired by: "Bedroom in Arles" Vincent Van Gogh, 1888, Musee D'orsay, Paris

THE MONEY SHOT

Over here. The sore spot. The wound.
A swath of downed firs, first growth.
And to the left—gouged hillside.

The scab is not healing;
It is not a matter of time.

South you'll find marble mines
Sand pits, copper, nickel, silver, prime
Land abandoned to fast food, burgers.

It doesn't rain in the rainforest anymore.

But wait, here's the money shot:

Ocean vista – wave spray. Delight of photo mags.
Jagged peaks, Alpine meadow overflows
Red poppies, orange calendula, wild radish
Houndstooth, Love in a Mist, Farewell to Spring, Wild Iris.

Take a shot.
It's free
While supplies last.

JOAN GELFAND

GLASS BUOYS

Convinced that her life is a dress rehearsal, my sister
Leaves foggy coast, flies to Thailand every January.

The wide, silty Mekong /ferries / the occasional dead body
Life, flowing just outside her small bamboo hut.

Her husband has pretty much stopped speaking
Except for essentials, communiqués like his boat's coded

Missives, informing the captain of weather, seafaring
Problems. Free diving, he hunts the ocean for booty

While my sister drifts, tangled in Japanese fishing line,
Butting up against glass buoys, devoured by shark,

Bobbing with unnamed desire, yearning for the next act,
Howling for her cosmic director to enter, to yell: CUT!

MOTHER'S DAY

When the train pulled out
Of 34th street station
Heading uptown,

The dense crowd vibrated
The third rail, naked
Bulbs. The grimy platform
Almost quaint
Some might even say
A festive atmosphere was in the air.

There were all those mothers being loved.
Looked to as the world in child's eyes
Even the conductor cracked
A smile, somewhere in the darkness
Between 38th and 41st,

But under the lights of 42nd Street
Something fell—luminous but odd
The shape of an arm
A leg, like someone diving
Without grace.

He blinked
Then blinked again
Felt something
Corporeal go under.

The people in the station turned pale.
In the next hours
Daughters heard

That mother had finally done
That which she had been dying to do.

Trains stopped dead
Along the A line.
Murmurs in the crowd

Suicide.

That train was her salvation.
The rat-filled tracks,
Ancient wheels, the rusty,
Bitter end
To a charmed and terrible life.

She'd had it all.
College when few could afford the fee,
An apartment in New York City.
The husband, and not one, but three
Exceptional children.

But everything wasn't enough
As pathways didn't light up
And those train lights called to her
Like home.

SECTION TWO

Ars Poetica

The Ferlinghetti School of Poetics

"All that we see, or seem, is but a
dream within a dream."
Edgar Allen Poe

I: The dream within the dream within the dream

What is it, Ferlinghetti,
Taking star turns in my dreams?
Strolling in front of cars
Haunting alleyways, stairways,
Bars? Beating moth like flitting through
San Francisco's sex fraught avenues? In North Beach
Where XXX marks art and
Nasty commerce collide, intersect Columbus,
Telegraph Hill, Jack Kerouac Way.
You are fog whispering in from the sea
On another sunny day.

"There's a breathless hush on the freeway tonight,
Beyond the ledges of concrete/Restaurants fall into dreams
With candlelight couples/Lost Alexandria still burns."

Ferlinghetti's words sink, weighted
On the business end of an invisible fishing line,
Dredging last night's dream to surface, gasping for air
Shivering like some catfish
Eyes bulging, wet lake water dripping off its scales.
The knife of memory slices open
That dream, finds me on haunted streets,
Instructing small boy:

"You gotta go to the Ferlinghetti school. It's totally rad
and completely cool."

II: Ferlinghetti Makes an Appearance

Phantom audience shouts: "Higher! Higher!"
Egg the poets on—after all, they're not on the wire.
Higher? We spin the memory wheel until there's my father
Strolling through his own Coney Island
And there he is again winning a goldfish
The clerk hands it over fish circling in plastic bag
Big Daddy pretends
It's all for the kids.
He needed to win like that fish needed water.

III: The Poet Reconsiders

Is the skill of life just keeping on
All the gears oiled, the doors open?
Even if the past keeps drowning and the knifed open
Dream fish still swims around?

In dream theater Ferlinghetti arrives.
Was it the Regal, the Royal or the Metreon?
I rise to make room for he who started everything
Got the wheel of poetry turning, broke
Open language, letters. Vaporized
While he drifts
Haunting my dreams.

*From "Wild Dreams of A New Beginning" by L. Ferlinghetti

I Know Why Sylvia Plath Put Her Head In The Oven

That morning Ted packed his briefcase.
Drove with a poet's gravity
Over the mountain
Of dishes. The sinking
Feeling. Leftovers. That morning
She woke up on the bathroom floor.

She woke with snatches of poetry
And a raging head but the babies needed breakfast
And poems evaporated like English fog
Lifting off the Devon trees.

The oven.
It was the confluence of things.

It was the confluence and coincidence
Everything gone wrong.
She'd been frightened,
And losing too long.

She'd been losing when she was supposed to be winning
All those long years between eight and thirty.
College, scholarships, but
She misplaced things. And, besides
She missed her daddy.

Besides, how should one live with Ted?
Complete the competing desires for a little madness,
The sublime? The constant need need need

As he dreams of Alissa, his well paid job
While staring at babies, burnt toast, tea cups?

Burnt toast and tea cups,
She ponders working,
But still, the wine glasses, the spills,
The laundry piled as nasty as traffic.

The Devon fog, the lost poems
The morning and the laundry,
The futility of it all.

WHILE I AM WRITING

While I am writing San Pancho sizzles
Cockatoo shivers hibiscus branch
Orange flowers tremble.
Babbled bird conversation,
Sky calling, sun seducing,
So distracting.

While I am writing in San Pancho,
Black chicken tiptoes
Into yard. Shrugs. Cackles.
Birds whistle. Low thrum
Delivered from static radio, television,
Mothers scolding.

While I am writing in San Pancho,
Netti instructs Suzanne in guitar fingerings
Charms with Latin songs of longing
Plays with Spanish inflection,
Great and total affection.

While I am writing in San Pancho
Trucks bounce on cobbled street
Wrecked shocks, megaphone
Hawks "Agua Puro! Camerones! Flogas!"

While I am writing in San Pancho,
The Pacific pounds, white sand
Bakes. Coco fronds, a debutante's skirt, rustle.
Frigate birds swoop, swallows dive,
Parrots sing "Hasta! Hasta!"

While I am writing in San Pancho,
Haiti digs out its dead
Searches collapsed structures, howls

Its loss. While I am writing in San Pancho
The world is living and turning
And loving and shaking
Yelling and birthing
Selling and buying.
Living and dying.

Go – Kart

Chained to neighbor's fence
Faded red hood coated in years
Of grease and road dust
Smell of hot asphalt
Summer afternoons.

Wrapped in fog shroud, a chill summer evening
Cable car rings its sweet bell
Open mic poems at Gallery café
Echo a symphony of varied and crazy tones.

I think I'm where I want to be.

Still, summer memories tug
A go-kart chained to a fence.

Poets House Walk

Across Brooklyn in a city dense
With watery dreams, a procession
Of crazy lovers strikes out
To hear poetry recited mid-span.
Hum of traffic
Roars approval.

Toward DUMBO through the mist
Poets, strivers, drivers, divers
Graying groupies, gropers, head out
To see hundred-year-old Kunitz carouse.

We stalk poetry across the bridge
In a town distracted, manufacturing
Your next thrill, and your next.

But the jig is up.
Rain.
All readings canceled.

Bicycle tires tharump over
Old pocked, trampled wood.
Rush of water slaps girders
Shivers of bridge as the last wet drop
Shatters metal decking.

Finally, showers surrender
To June light, shadow slant
Wide angles of cable, long stripes
Falling across beaten planks
A gorgeous geometry,
Engineering, poetry, and the wonder
Of holding things aloft.

*DownUnderManhattanBridge

Meeting Milosz

Called in to inspect the drafts
I am the expert
Arrive, blue
Collar outside
Poet's soul disguised

The Nobel's request:
"Keep the heat in
The cold out.
    Make it tight."

I survey the English
Cottage, creeping ivy,
Leaded glass windows,
Picture book gables
The mezzanine's
Miles and miles of books
Tomes in lost languages.
I search out air pockets,
Means of escape.

Hear the embattled terrain
The earth traversed, the poet's travail
In each square inch of the
Leaking home.

Milosz signs,
With zero interest
In disappearing ink.

Esteemed poet
Wants what everybody wants.
Low electric bills,
A house in the hills.

The long view.

Open Mic

the local, the express-
ive, the out-of-towner
the LA writer screening
his calls the visiting professor
the visionary/game designer
screaming puns and algorithms
the Bean Towner, the Londoner

The self-appointed NY crown Prince
Street Cornelia café.
The scene the beauty queen
The well-heeled,
The tragically hip, the perennially
Needy, the studiously disheveled

The earnest
The ruminating
The published
The pissed off
The ironic

The notebook readers
The under-medicated
The bi-polar bisexual
The trannies, the wanna-be's

The homies, the hoodies
The hungry, the feeders
The doodlers, the pray-ers
The homeless, the homespun

The uncomfortable
The too comfortable
The speed talkers
The fire walkers

Foot soldiers in Poetry's army
Flak jackets, steel helmets, x-ray goggles
Staring at empty pockets
Corralling the angels and their minions
Serving up the first word, and the last.

For: Connie and Kit and Cher and Philip and Clive & all the open mic saints

SECTION THREE

Taste

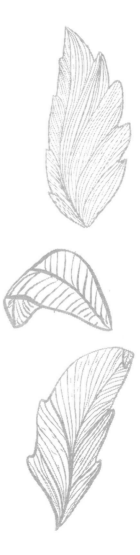

Russian River Watershed

Russian River floods, then trickles
Burst from serpentine, Mayacamas
Through valley haze flows
West always west.

Until word spreads:
Volcanic soil makes very good
Grapevines; sells higher
Than Pink Ladies, Braeburns,
Gravensteins, Taylor's Gold.

Vineyards.

Apple trees topple like mown weeds
Their imperfect limbs ripe with rosy fruit
Meaty walnuts, apricots, plums
Pears and figs plowed under,
River flow diverted.
California churns tree trunks
As the world clamors for Cabernet,
Pinot Noir. Farmers hoe,
Gird for another Gold Rush.

Vineyards.

Trees pulled as fast as oil
Siphoned from southern deserts,
As violently as veins were mined.

Merlot, Chardonnay, Sauvignon Blanc
Replace apple's knobby arms, the shady glen.

Who's to sip this pricey lode?

Blue-black oak-studded hills
Replaced by purple grapes hanging ripe.

Scatter them. They matter to birds,
Hungry mouths.

Paris Whistling

Birdlike notes ricochet through quiet Quarter,
A mynah's hopeful love call.
Man whistles, long coat
Buttoned against late fall chill.

One note runs up and down the scale of his heart's desire.
The singular music follows him like sunlight, breaking fire.
Does he think of his wife who will kiss him kindly at the door?
Or, perhaps, last night, or the night before?
Has he just enjoyed an excellent cassoulet, a crisp Sancerre?
Heading home, Parisian men whistle everywhere.

Songs counterpoint screech and rumble of Metro.
The men whistle, strolling from Tuesday market,
A basket of currants cradled as carefully as a newborn,
Or fruit for a fresh tart, the juicy center of a crepe.

When did we forget to teach our children
To lick their lips and pucker?

Whistling.

When did it become passé
To share a tiny slice of happiness,
Wear your heart on your sleeve?

Bumper Crop

Peaches are cheap this summer
Ninety-nine cents a pound
Juicy sweet, complex and round.

The globes are just so gorgeous
Inspiring jams and compotes,
Crumbles, crisps and pies.

One bite and everything turns right.

Is it a trick of fate
We're eating peaches
And feeling oh-so-fine?

As wars rage, earthquakes shake
Tsunamis deluge, hurricanes destroy?
Is it a ruse that peaches grow?
A trick? A plot? A ploy?

Bumper crop. That's what we got.
There is no rhyme, or reason.
It's just what we receive
In a very good season.

ODE TO TOAST

Let's toast toast the bread we roast -
The best burnt thing I have ever known.
Let's toast the aroma that rouses a dog
From its coma, the waft of comfort
And sustenance, the sweet smell
That courses from morning to shape up our day.

Let's toast heat and cooking and making
Something out of nothing.
Let's toast the toaster while we're at it
Raise a glass in honor of skinny wire coils
That heat out bread's best.

Finally, let's toast Tesla's mother
And her Napa marmalade: cooked down apricots,
That taste of sun that lightly loves but never smothers.
French butter on top of toast.

Let's toast coffee in bed while we're on the subject of breakfast.

Yes!

CAFÉ

I never intended to fritter an afternoon
Espresso in hand, beret cocked to the left.
It's simply a posture much too obvious.
Too Sartre and deBeauvoir. Too poseur.
But in spring, logic takes a hike with reason
And common sense gets on the bus
Leaving us stranded at the intersection of High and Falutin.
Like a spring storm, without warning,
I long for the peripheral scrim of conversation -
The burst of sun on someone else's awning. Mothers strolling,
Pushing babies yawning, toddlers riding bikes. I'm in the swell,
The beautiful wave of budding humanity.
I blend in handily: as necessary as the grocery.
I'm a backdrop, part of the scenery, a fount of industry
To be noticed and not noticed. Like the newly leaved willow
Singing full throated to the April breeze.

NATURE MORTE AU PANIER

Pears. Various. Ripe.
D'anjou, Bosc, Forelle, Comice.
Round, not round laid bare
In family's frayed basket.
Linen cloth, open jug. Light.

"Nature Morte Au Panier," by Cezanne hangs in the Musee D'Orsay/Paris.

JOAN GELFAND

Lime Tanka

Lime drizzled on papaya
Lime squeezed into icy cerveza
Lime drenched snapper
Sour sweet citrus fresh
Taste times joyous

SECTION FOUR

SeX. Death. And All That Jazz

MUSIC: DREAM SEVEN

Sing to me in sotto voce.
Sing rings around me like a tree's
Rings show history, the years.

Carbon date me as you sing a ring around
My planet. I am Saturn, and you are a red
Vaporous ring mysteriously circling.

Sing to me a cappella. Your voice
Hugs my body weaves its way
Like a needle through unknown fabric.
Your voice calls to me, slices like a ray
Of light exposing dark places.

Sing to me in a voice, deep.
Lull me, rock me, call me "baby."
Take me on your journey of desire and fantasy.
Piece me back together with your sharp tongue.
Cry out for me in a voice, warm as the sun.

Sing to me of things you will not say,
In rhythm and rhyme,
Sing to me in three-quarter time.

Making Love In An Empty Apartment

Across the courtyard (crisp air,
Windows shut tight)
Making love in an empty apartment,
A couple I do not know.

The curtains are packed, the boxes shipped
The dishes wrapped. The furniture sold, or donated.

Tuesday morning. I'm caught
By autumn slant sunlight, shadow on buttocks,
The impression of windowpanes stretching
Across bodies pulsing like passing bridge girders.

Is it ceremonious?
Or perhaps, a simple affirmation of life
In all that emptiness?

Or is it the final pull of lovers
While chance and life are pulling them apart?

VALENTINE'S DAY

Cupid's army woke up
On the wrong side of the bed.
Shot a shower of arrows helter-skelter.
Hearts were slashed, lives were razed.
All the wrong people were falling in love.

Call it global warming, climate change
The darts flew willy-nilly.
Married fell in love with married
Single with married, old with young.

Mothers tied yellow ribbons around baby carriages
Brides-to-be pulled the wedding veil close
To protect from Cupid's mayhem.
Still, souls collided and worlds divided
When Cupid struck us broadside.

We felt an ache as the small bones,
The ones that protect heart from hurt,
Front and back, cracked.
Pierced arrows angled
When Cupid blinked
And Love, his mercurial agent, ran amok.

PARIS KISSES

Top steps, le Metro
A bedroom kiss.
On the Champs-Elysees,
On the escalier,
On line at L'Orangerie,
The Tuilleries, on the quay.
Kisses are a greeting, a sign,
Part of the landscape, as ancient as barky tree.

They're kissing on Rive Gauche, the Ile St.Louis.
Those kisses light the lights,
Shimmy up the Tour Eiffel
Turning hard steel into giant sparkler
Pulsing with delight, burning with joy.
Kisses light the Bateau Mouche sailing on soft curvature
Of ink-black Seine, painting
Orangey, warm reflections.

Paris kisses. It's the embrace,
The sensual meeting.
Bonjour! Au Revoir! And
Everything in between.
Kisses: They're catching, contagious.
Divine.

So, don't just there, mon cher!
Start the street fair,
The praying, the vigor, the leap,
Start that engine to roil
The blood, the veins to boil
Start those birds to singing
The flags to swinging
Start that sweetness and all that's delicious
Start the drinking, the eating, start those
Paris kisses!

Sex. Death. And All That Jazz

In one night love gripped
Time was suspended
And the love was the love of the contented.

Soon after, the firing squad arrived.
Gunned down innocent soldiers.
My heart stopped, it ached, crying out
For the men and all their mothers.

Sex and death are closest relatives; one lives upstairs,
One lives down. The furniture is the same but different;
Sex prefers overstuffed chairs in shades of red,
Death digs on black, clean lines, a wooden bed.

Sex and death share walls and floors and
Sometimes when you're held by love
You can hear death taking the stairs, one by one by one.
It's a fragile co-existence, this. Sex. Death.
And all that jazz.

Sex and death, and all that jazz – it's anything but mellow.
It's about the shake up, the shake down, the shaky boots and more
It's about the flip-flop stomach, the flight of bees.
The shock of the right fellow, the weak knees.

Sex, death and all that jazz.
We never stop to realize,
That like a good story,
The beginning is in the end.

GRAVE

Side by side lie two
Most illustrious thinkers:
Spare white marble, cold.

In the Montparnasse cemetery: the graves of Simone deBeauvoir and Jean Paul Sartre

THE MARRIAGE EGG

We begin:
Soft, gelatinous,
A savory soup of hope.

Your cloudy white divided
Just barely, by my sunny yolk.

The thinnest membrane
Divides translucent frames.
A tender nudge
Sets our insides to gush.

Over time
(much boiling water, heat)
We solidify.

There are boundaries.

Now, what once cracked
With the slightest tap
Calcified. It is our home.

We live inside this marriage egg,
The yolk, the white
Clearly defined.

Inside our hard
But fragile shell.

La Dolce Vida

In the movie, square-jawed hero grabs platinum-helmeted heroine.
She falls into him like she's been waiting since creation to give herself
away. She melts into lust with easy, nubile ecstasy. In the movie, our
girl doesn't need hot baths, long talks, many glasses of champagne,
jewelry, diamonds, rare wine.
There's no time!

In the movie, our heroine requires just a violin, not much enticement.
Not even a poem.
The tabloids have the kiss on file.
Our young girls deconstruct the scenes: Platinum, blond, ash blond,
dirty blond, tall, long-legged, narrow-waisted. They secretly muse:
why don't I fall?

When all they want is not to be noticed, but seen? And so they starve
themselves, they cut, they flour the plumbing with their guts.
They are distant, confused, depressed, and certainly not aroused!

They have no urge to throw themselves into anyone's arms. They
worry about love which, for their money, is a slow blooming, or a
good storm brewing off the coast.
What they know of love is not that movie, that kiss. And not that
surrender.

It's something mysterious, something fleeting and something much
more tender.

Scraping Dead Stars Off the Pavement

Japanese Maple Tanka

Leaf upon leaf, dense
Paper-thin petals sheer as
Shadow behind shade
A bouquet of fine tissue
Green delight for tired eyes.

Joan Gelfand

Overheard @ Venice Beach

Mid-recession, a downright depression.
Washington calls it a "slow down."
Tell that to the guys huddled downtown
In doorways and bus shelters
In city offices trying to pull ends together
Match up need with funds.

Still, it is Saturday on Venice beach.
Morning sun. Silent, stationed roller coaster,
Under boardwalk, north to Malibu, Zuma. past Palisades,
Overheard: "I'll sell a quarter of a million."

Tourist wife watches bikes, skaters glide by.
Thinks but doesn't say 'looks like fun.' On the sidelines
Junkies and funky people settling up tabs, setting up stalls
Euro strollers. African, Indian conduct business, tender
And not so legal in front of "Grass Roots Pot Club." Rolling
Joints under brilliant fantastic mural of dolphins, surf bums,
Rollerbladers, in-line skaters, hibernators,
Proscrastinors, prognosticators.

Venice: melange of movie queens, hedge fund men;
Producer and producer and producer.
And that fabulous
Southern California sun
Shining
On everyone.

BEACH FLOWERS

Carpets of purple, hard-won
Blooms suffer fog, bitter breezes
Crappy soil. Beach flowers fend off
Encroachers, dog shit, bird droppings,
Cat's paws, joggers, mountain bikes,
Strollers, do-good marathons.

Friend of salt, sea spray, seal's bark, windy nights,
Ice plant reclines, spilling lavender happiness
Across this foggy county
Just so that the one day sunshine breaks
Through cloud cover, it bursts
Vibrant and new
Resistant to all who traverse,
Pounce, and trounce.
The sturdy flower, survives.

BLUE MOON

This blue moon's lost
Behind east facing hills
Her brightness, dulled
Obscured face.
She's chaste.

December's blue moon wanders
Out of site. Is she veiled,
A tragic Desdemona,
Mourning for penguins,
Polar bears?

Spinning somewhere in a black hole
Is she wild? Out of control?

I surrender hope
Of glimpsing her dinner plate face,
The warm milky smile.

Succumb to scraping dead stars
Off the pavement
So many light years below.

Tassa Hanalei

Study the architecture of banana trees
The angle and arch of leaves
And the arc of a raindrop
As it slips
Noiselessly
Onto lush pillow
Of fallen leaf.
Decode the musicology of a waterfall
Its icy tones and samba rhythms
Basso timbre.
Observe the flight patterns of egrets
Long white necks stretched
Outward, toward landings.
Feel warm breezes.
Your hand in my hand.
As the world shifts
Into day and night is blurred
By sleep and love.

COBRA SONNET

Darlingtonia Californica is no sweetie of mountain species
A plant as graceful as milkmaid's pitcher,
She hides among tall trees
Where she munches on bugs and innocents.
A slim seductress of the creek
She's called Cobra plant; her form, compels, and then deceives.

Her colors draw greedy flies, her flower ever enticing.
Pod sprouts next to gurgling creeks.
Never naïve, this lover is vicious
Attracts bugs to her sticky sweetness, trapped, succumb
And Darlingtonia's carnivorous dinner, quickly become.

Nestled among shooting stars, hound's tongue
Leopard lilies, bleeding hearts and foxglove –
High up above tree line, near knife sharp peaks
Alive in mountain's chill
Our darling Darlingtonia is the only plant that kills.

She's rare and famous, Darlingtonia. Feasts on skeeter carcass
While wrens steer clear and even tiresome jays traverse
Sideways, long ways, search out the furthest thermal
In northern Trinity Alps' jagged, landscape.

Our Cobra plant lives where angels
Swim in crystal water, playing, skipping and jiving
Where lemon sage scents the air and hummingbirds dive-
Bomb fuchsias and monkey flowers for nectar so divine.

In this pristine meadow, in this place so close to heaven,
Darlingtonia Californica, our deadly beauty, thrives.

The Summer I Learned to Love the Fog

Through foggy filter
Steely ocean
Is a grey plate

No reflection
The sun's absorbed

The entire light spectrum

Into this beautiful
Muted summer

September Fifteenth

In one week, summer closes up shop
Pull the shutters, mow the yellowed lawn.
From now on, things will be different.
The pond will freeze, the lake too cold
The forest's fecundity will go numb.
The visiting will stop - too far to drive.
Ferries are docked. We'll survive.

Now, we enter Equinox
When sun and moon, poised
Cease rotation, equal for a moment
Before the scales tip
And even Indian summer can't breathe
Life back into the dying light.

SECTION SIX

Practice

YOGA

Pigeon poses problems.
The particular angle of calf to thigh
The troubles secreted
Inside knotty tendon,
Ache of gnarled hamstring.
Stored sadness.

Bend, curl, fold —
Abrade the unnamable.
I return to pigeon like a child worrying a scab,
Exposing fresh wound

Until I am pigeon, roosting
Mottled, sturdy and grey.
I become a landed bird
Perennially homing, homing.

5:50 AM

Morning. Layer of mist
Night streetlights still lit
Neighbor flicks on kitchen
Overhead, winter birds scatter
From nests. We are the restless
The night shift going home.

Square-shaped Latin woman lugs
Two shopping bags, lumbers
Toward #44 O'Shaughnessy.
We are the silent ones,
Hurtling through urban landscape
Slowly waking, driving toward the cushion
Where we will sit upright, poised,
Alert. One foot on earth, one in sky -
A quiet sangha of five -
Alive, on the knife-edge of creation.

GREEN DRAGON ZENDO

Four torsos shadowed
My head, shoulders just like yours
In a line, human.

THREE POEMS ABOUT NOTHING

I: The Nun In Me

The nun in me isn't very pure.
Quite the opposite. This paramour
Is a nasty seductress shaking
Up decadent cocktails of vice.

The nun in me isn't very nice.
Wandering out late, scheming,
Skating with an ethereal lover,
A faceless man with sexy moves,
Her shadowy full moon accomplice.

The nun in me isn't very devoted.
Running plotting against every angel
Who seems an obvious guide. Wanting, wanton
Stuffed full of wine and avarice.

The nun in me behaves badly.
In fact she's better on her own where there's no one to push,
No fights to incite.
She's not very good at marriage,
To be precise.

Still, the nun in me craves a warm fire, her devoted spouse
And loves her all-black kitty. She imagines her little family wildly
careening
Like sightless bats through a long, dark tunnel
Flying by feeling, sensing the way home.

II: The "Nun" in me

Hebrew letters are numbers
And the inverse of the obverse is true.
The Torah is duality; calligraphed black

And all of the white space too.
And Nun has just my number—it's fifty
Fruitful and vibrant,

The gate of faith itself.

III: The "None" in me

Am I empty enough? A circle with no center?
I want nothing, really, except everything
And in small doses, and all at once.
Is the none in me empty enough?
I've said my prayers, sat on my cushion,
I've stayed alert and relaxed.

Is the none in me empty enough?
Wasn't it you who told me
The world was seamless
And that went for the lampshade too.

Later, you apologized but why?
Was that before or after you said you loved me
Once? In this lifetime,
Once was just enough.

Am I empty enough yet?
The everything
In me become the 'none?'

* "Nun" letter in the Hebrew alphabet

THE PRAISE TANKA

After thirteen hours in the zendo
Incense offerings, prostrations
The Sutras and the daisho
I am empty—for a moment

For Rabbi Alan Lew

The Lake Takes the Place of a Heart

"A lake is different from a pond."
"Oh, yes?"
"Yes, a lake has water coming in, and going out."
"Like a heart."

I: Water In

This year, surface waters are icy cold,
Deep waters—warmer.

II: Water Out

It was a hard year.
All those granite thrusts
Millennia of upsurge, shifting crusts
The lake takes the place of a heart.

III: Water In

We got there the long way
Hauled up dusty rock trail
Scratched by bushberries, thornapple, bramble.
Arrived at the lake shaped like a heart.

Blood in. Blood out.

IV: *There is no idea but in things.*

This thing, this lake, this softness
Beats mercifully. Hugs nakedness. Wrings out loss,
Washes fear with snowmelt,
Embraces skin. Scours edges.

Water in. Water out.

Dive deep.
Lose sound.
Go down with fish and muck
Dirt and scum, petrified
Rock. Emerge into Sierra sunlight
High blue altitude
Open
Sky.

There is no idea but in things.
William Carlos Williams – from "Paterson 1"

Haystacks in Snow

Weak winter light
Day's end or
A pale sunrise
Reflected barn side.

Haystacks in snow,
The early light,
The late light,
In that moment
Before night falls,
Before day begins.

Inspired by Monet's "Haystacks in Snow"

Joan Gelfand

DAY LONG

All day sit zazen
I love you. Not personal
I love birds, trees too.

I'm in the Whole Foods natural medicine you-can-cure-anything department when I find myself smack in front of a shelf of tiny bottles promising no less than magic.

I imagine the tiny brown bottles manufactured by tiny elves dressed in tiny green organic cotton outfits, the herbs gathered by said tiny elves in outrageously beautiful fields somewhere in Northern California.

Agrimony

"The jovial, cheerful, humorous people who love peace and are distressed by argument or quarrel, to avoid which they will agree to give up much. Though generally they have troubles and are tormented and restless and worried in mind or in body, they hide their cares behind their humor and jesting and are considered very good friends to know. They often take alcohol or drugs in excess, to stimulate them and help themselves bear their trials with cheerfulness."

It's ok if I take two, right?

Aspen

"Vague unknown fears, for which there can be given no explanation, no reason. It is a terror that something awful is going to happen even though it is unclear what exactly. These vague inexplicable fears may haunt by night or day. Sufferers may often be afraid to tell their trouble to others."

I'll take it.

Chestnut Bud

"For those who take a longer time than others to learn the lessons of daily life. Whereas one experience would be enough for some, such people find it necessary to have more, sometimes several, before the lesson is learnt. Therefore, to their regret, they find themselves having to make the same error on different occasions when once would have been enough, or observation of others could have spared them even that one fault."

Now I have three.

Edging away from the shelf of magic, I sneak just one last peek!

Elm

"Those who are doing good work, are following the calling of their life and who hope to do something of importance, and this often for the benefit of humanity. At times there may be periods of depression when they feel that the task they have undertaken is too difficult, and not within the power of a human being."

Ahem. Does Bach intend us to treat all these symptoms at once, or serially?
Is this a day long process, a week, a year?
Can I safely mix all the tiny bottles, the magic potions?
I search for contraindications!
FDA warnings? Surgeon General's treatise on herbs and avoiding magic elves while pregnant or in the presence of high blood pressure!

What would happen if I mix all three?
Would Chestnut Bud cancel out Aspen?
Would learning life lessons more quickly cancel out a comfort with new confidences?

Impatiens

"Those who are quick in thought and action and who wish all things to be done without hesitation or delay. When ill they are anxious for a hasty recovery. They find it very difficult to be patient with people who are slow as they consider it wrong and a waste of time, and they will Endeavour to make such people quicker in all ways. They often prefer to work and think alone, so that they can do everything at their own speed."

There's a cure for that?

I'm standing there, juggling five tiny bottles.
Agrimony, Aspen, Impatiens, Elm and Chestnut Bud. Finally. Cures for my ailing, aching soul.

I close my eyes – trying to imagine a self-medication exercise.

In one scenario: I'm leaving Whole Foods with an armload of tiny bottles and about $100 poorer.

I imagine myself taking all at once, a magic cocktail if you will,
Praying for absolution from ambition, impatience, fear, anxiety, terror.

Outside, the day grows warmer. I need more time. Wait – that was Aspen, right? Or was it Agrimony?

I'm re-reviewing the entire inventory when paralysis, familiar, yet comforting, takes hold.

No decision could be a good decision, right? Things have a way of working themselves out.

Don't they?

SECTION SEVEN

Epilogue

Post Mortem

After seven days
Stalking verbs, phrases
Nouns and similes
Like a tourist on safari

She arrives home to the tribe

Dried out plants
The cat's bowl, empty

She hauls laundry,
Garbage, take-out containers
Combats strange smells.

After a week of breathing
Mountain misery a sense
Of home in the wide open
She faces closed up rooms
Windows locked
And a certain gym sock
Aroma permeating the bedroom.

Did Odysseus suffer so?

It tries her sense of humor
As she cleans up the mess,
But after scrubbing the refrigerator,
Tossing moldy food
She loses her cool

When finally
She misses her mother
Who taught her how
To run a tight ship,

Taught her how to row.

Acknowledgements

"Good Morning America, Where Are You?" Fighting Words, PEN Oakland Anthology, 2013, Continent of Light, (2011/anthology), New Verse News (webzine) (Winter, 2010), OccuPoetry: 2011, 99 Blog, edited by Dean Rader. "99 Poems" Edited by Dean Rader

"The Ferlinghetti School of Poetics," Poets 11: 2010, Sparring With Beatnik Ghosts, 2013 Anthology, Archived at Bancroft Library, UC Berkeley, Du Page Valley Review, Winter, 2011; Bay Area Seasonal Poetry Review, Fall 2010. Levure Litteraire, Paris

"Café," Poets 11: 2010 and Song of the San Joaquin

"5:50 AM" Poets 11: 2010

"Bach Flower Remedies" It's Animal But Merciful, Anthology, greatweatherforMEDIA.com, NYC, 2012

"Valentine's Day" – The Griffin, Fall 2012 and Caveat Lector: Winter, 2012

"I Know Why Sylvia Plath Put Her Head in the Oven" gape-seed, Anthology, Uphook Press, NY, Fall 2011

"The Lake Takes The Place of a Heart," New Grass, California Poets in the Schools anthology, 2011

"Paris Kisses," in Love Poetry Chapbook published by the City of Benicia, CA, 2011

"Russian River Watershed," Broken Circles: A Gathering of Poems for Hunger, Anthology, Cave Moon Press, Yakima, Washington: 2011

"Music: Dream Seven" Touching: Poems of Love, Longing and Desire, Fearless Books Press, Berkeley, 2011

"Lime Tanka" California Quarterly, California State Poetry Society, 24th Annual Anthology, 2011

"Go-Kart" Song of the San Joaquin Quarterly, August 2010

"Tassa Hanalei," and "Haystacks in Snow" Ambush #1, Fall 2010

"Paris Whistling" The Gathering Ten, 2009 Ina Coolbrith Circle Anthology

"Poets House Walk" Connections: New York Bridges in Poetry anthology, P&Q Press 2012

Beatrice.com, June 2010

"Making Love in an Empty Apartment" The Toronto Quarterly, Volume 4, Spring 2010

"Sex. Death. And All That Jazz," Winningwriters.com, Spring, 2010, Caveat Lector Fall 2009

"Nature Morte Au Panier," The Light in Ordinary Things, Anthology, Fearless Books, September, 2009

"Japanese Maple Tanka" Osmosis Sanctuary, July, 2009

"Three Poems About Nothing" Marin Poetry Center Anthology Fall 2009

"Marriage Egg," "Paris Whistling," "Who Will Immortalize You?" Building Bridges from Writers to Readers, San Francisco Writers Conference Anthology, 2009

"Ode To Toast" Betty's List, Fall 2009

Awards/Nominations

Honorable Mention: Benicia Love Poetry Contest, February 2011 for "Paris Kisses"

Touching: Poems of Love, Longing and Desire: Winner in the Anthology category AND Second Place Grand Prize Winner in the Nonfiction category in the 2011 Next Generation Indie Book Awards. It has also been named Winner of the Poetry Category in Dan Poynter's inaugural Global e-Book Awards. (Anthology includes "Music: Dream Seven")

Honorable Mention/Pen Women – Roanoke Valley Branch, Fall 2010: "I Know Why Sylvia Plath Put Her Head in the Oven."

California State Poetry Society, 24th Annual Contest, January 2011: "Lime Tanka"

Food Poetry Contest, Cave Moon Press, 2011 "Russian River Watershed"

Poets 11, 2010, District 7, San Francisco, CA. Jack Hirshman, Juror. "Ferlinghetti School of Poetics," "Café," "5:50 AM"

Osmosis Sanctuary/July 2009 Best Poem "Japanese Maple Tanka"

Thanks!

Thank you to my publishers, especially Benicia Literary Arts, greatweatherformedia.com, Carol Smallwood, Christopher Bernard, Christopher Gortner, Linda Joy Myers and Sari Friedman. Thanks also to Poets & Writers for grants to support readings in Davis, Point Arena and Detroit. Thank you to my publicist, Kim McMiillon, my friends and colleagues in Wom-ba, the Women's National Book Association, the Women's Poetry Salon as well as the Diane Middlebrook Salon in San Francisco. Thank you to Rebecca Foust for being an early reader and scrupulous editor. And thank you to all of my poetry boosters: Connie Post, Kit Kennedy, Stephen Kopel, Dan Brady, Deborah Grossman, Yvonne Campbell, Lucy Lang Day, Marty Castleberg, Meg Waite Clayton, Vicki Weiland, Ruth Hertz, Debbie Kinney, Renate Stendahl, Geoffrey Katz, Jane Ormerod, Susan Stanger, Emily Klion, Lindsay Hertz, Crystal Yang, Drea Woodard, and George Brooks.

Thank you also to my teachers: Judy Behr; poet and Zen master, Norman Fischer; Rabbi Dorothy Richman and Micah Hyman.

With gratitude and love to my family, Simone Gelfand and my beloved, Adam Hertz.

About The Author

Joan's poetry, fiction, essays and reviews have been published in national and international publications. Joan teaches for Poetry Inside Out, is a member of the National Book Critics Circle & Poetry Editor for the "J." She also teaches High School Students the art of recitation for Poetry Out Loud, a program of the National Endowment for the Arts administrated by the California Arts Council.

President of the Women's National Book Association from 2008-1010, Joan is now the Development Chair for the organization. Joan blogs regularly for the Huffington Post.

Joan graduated Mills College with a Master of Fine Arts in Creative Writing and holds a Bachelor of Arts from San Francisco State in English with an emphasis in Creative Writing. A dynamic and passionate reader and speaker, Joan has read in venues around the US and Mexico. She is a regular speaker at the San Francisco Writer's Conference and coaches writers.

To learn more about Joan, visit her website:
http://joangelfand.com
Like us on Facebook: www.facebook/longblueroom.com

CPSIA information can be obtained at www.ICGtesting.com
Printed in the USA
BVOW08s1200170214

345125BV00001B/6/P

9 780970 373724